The National Poetry Series w
publication of five collections ᵥ
five participating publishers. The Series is funded annually by
Amazon Literary Partnership, Betsy Community Fund, Gettinger
Family Foundation, Bruce Gibney, HarperCollins Publishers,
Stephen King, Lannan Foundation, Newman's Own Foundation,
Anna and Olafur Olafsson, O. R. Foundation, PG Family
Foundation, Poetry Foundation, Elise and Steven Trulaske,
and the National Poetry Series Board of Directors.

2018 COMPETITION WINNERS

Fear of Description by **Daniel Poppick**
Chosen by Brenda Shaughnessy for Penguin Books

Valuing by **Christopher Kondrich**
Chosen by Jericho Brown for University of Georgia Press

Eyes Bottle Dark with a Mouthful of Flowers by **Jake Skeets**
Chosen by Kathy Fagan for Milkweed Editions

It's Not Magic by **Jon Sands**
Chosen by Richard Blanco for Beacon Press

Nervous System by **Rosalie Moffett**
Chosen by Monica Youn for Ecco

VALUING

CHRISTOPHER KONDRICH

The University of Georgia Press
Athens

The epigraph by Simone Weil is from *Simone Weil: An Anthology*, copyright © 1986 by Sian Miles. Used by permission of Grove Atlantic, Inc., and Little, Brown. Any third party use of this material, outside of this publication, is prohibited. The line "the only evil consists . . . in a deficit of existence," appearing in the poem "Bellfounding," is from from Georgio Agamben, *The Coming Community*, translated by Michael Hardt (Minneapolis University of Minnesota Press, 1993), p. 44, and was originally published in Italian in *La comunità che viene*, copyright 1990 Einaudi, Turin; English translation copyright 1993 by the Regents of the University of Minnesota.

Designed by Erin Kirk New
Set in Arno and Lato
Printed and bound by Thomson-Shore, Inc.
The paper in this book meets the guidelines for permanence and durability of the Committee on Production Guidelines for Book Longevity of the Council on Library Resources.

Most University of Georgia Press titles are available from popular e-book vendors.

Printed in the United States of America
23   22   21   20   19   P   5   4   3   2   1

Library of Congress Cataloging-in-Publication Data
Names: Kondrich, Christopher, 1982– author.
Title: Valuing / Christopher Kondrich.
Description: Athens : The University of Georgia Press, 2019. |
Series: The National Poetry Series
Identifiers: LCCN 2019006690 | ISBN 9780820355702 (pbk. : alk. paper) |
ISBN 9780820355719 (ebook)
Classification: LCC PS3611.O58465 A6 2019 | DDC 811/.6—dc23
LC record available at https://lccn.loc.gov/2019006690

Contents

Everything without exception which is of value in me
comes from somewhere other than myself, not as a gift
but as a loan which must be ceaselessly renewed.

SIMONE WEIL

VALUING

Asylum

I choose to love the dawn; it speaks
in light. Long had its silence
silenced me. I choose to love this table
where I lie, the instruments that tell me
what I am made of. I am made
of things I love: the onlookers
peering over, trying to find some
what of them, maybe a gem or pencil
they once held. Maybe a vein
like their veins. Or their sleep.
I choose to love our auspices
because they brought us here, to love
disobedience because it shows the freedom
to love or not love. Or value. I choose
to value. I choose to love
as asylum from that which presses me
to hate. This body, which is not
a body. This representation, which is all
there is. I have a choice in the matter.
To touch you, I choose my hands.

Dwelling

It is alright. You may dwell in me. I am the conflagration
of the never-at-home and the never-not-at-home that makes you
part of the history of people. And though I have no holdings,
you may increase your stock in me;
you may reserve the right to vessel. To partition if you need to.
To live amongst walls and proclaim those walls a home. Even now
I have already clothed you in vanishing
numbers, which as they rise cluster in your not being
able to picture them as they are. Able to picture me without with,
without resemblance to prior dwelling,
which pulls at you now as you stand before me. Arms supporting
a door the way Mary supported Christ in pietà.

Orientation

To orient the mind one must orient the world.
I am facing north, but I am descending
into the blue and white lines of Puget Sound.
Rising up into the feeling of horizon.

My arms are my country's flags
staked to the spots where I've touched you.
Reaching up through the border,
you are younger than your body lets on.

Waves, waves of the Hudson River
are more like the creases of your voice. Erupting
from the Long Island Sound onto the banks
when the storm was just intention.

I come to you grieving, giving thanks, catching
in the trap with some birds. Why did you erect it?
Did you mean to catch more than a meal?
The morsels of my flesh are lessening

in your mouth, breaking down into the strings
of acceptance. I am only a matter
of time. When you revealed yourself
as leaves, I was already beginning to dissolve.

Division of Labor

I'm wondering if I would have tied obligation
to the wooden post of the dock if others hadn't already.
Mine goes certain and uncertain on little swells
the current makes dough of itself by kneading
with the heels of uninformed hands
lily pads with upturned edges ready to collect
themselves incrementally. I send a part
of myself from the boat to the village I read somewhere
can swallow an I not into a crowd but into buildings,
the *was constructed* of them, their *was here* and *loved*,
pleats into which an I can slip and fade
like water fades its temperateness to boiling. Which makes
my body whistle, the I in me whistles, not absent luck
or looseness, but through a fissure in the body
that's always there between reaching and touching,
the kind of fissure that makes the wall of me more apparent
and the whistle sting more. Through the wall
I watch my thought of looking up at the sail the wind
fell out of and decide to send another part
after the first, which, like the tail of a lizard, had grown back
to bend and in bending had proven able,
declared itself an ear to receive a call. Into village
it responded by moving into admitting into
its fragment the squares of on-the-surface I thought
beautiful from the boat, beyond the surface
were below-the-surface things like warble and treble
and a bar with wingback chairs
where the part I sent first was ordering a Manhattan,
not astonishing its piece into abeyance
but into ice cubes projecting memory it collected
like a bowerbird, something distant
that had happened on its way from the boat,

which was now one of many boats attributing to the dock
what they had learned from the ocean, that anything bobbing
bobs because of anything else. Although the boats were empty,
they had drifted together and were now each tapping
the dock on its shoulder, without question
a scene so solemn and tranquil I regretted sending it
with the third part of someone I no longer resembled,
which, I guess, was the point of the first part of me returning
the smell of bourbon in a felted wooden box where its
I had rested in the shape of itself
taking shape through the spiral of a French horn. I gestured
this part under the vinculum
where an empty boat was
waiting to be divided where the decimal sat
along the center thwart my first part mirrored to
without my face ever moving and before I intended
to untie the boat, it was and I had
left my second and third parts in the village
not knowing if it was light out or dark.

Geometry of Echo

It was like I had to own nothing
to part from it.

Give away my possessions
in order to leave nothing behind.

To own nothing is to see
the meaning in it.

The meaning that nothing provides.
Though if nothing has

a meaning, it is that it does things
nothing else can.

Nothing works that way.
I take comfort in this,

and then sell it.

Clearing

Never have we worshipped
so many suns:

the morning sun
with its golden tassels,

the evening sun
with its mask of moon,

the sun on the sea
of undulating eyes

that refract the giant eye
watching from space.

Remember when the ocean
was forest.

We used the big razor
to reveal a clearing

of water that could worship
for us.

Map of Belonging

In order to be immortal you have to be invisible to the part of you that knows you have to die. There is a story about this. In it, a crane grows to the size of a man's desire to evade death. Which is to say, large enough to carry him. To the city in the country of perpetual life, a kind of purgatory where money buys poison that doesn't work. Unlike the others, he is happy. Time has yet to swell in him like the crescendo of devastating music. He spends his days dusting in the replica of his house. The bowl overturned like the shell of a turtle. The butter dish, a trough or like a river escorting knees. *Am I getting older*, he asks, *if my body doesn't age?* The menagerie of others looks to him for new ideas. *What about this poker—is it sharp enough to pierce?* It is and it isn't, they discover. Then the man and the others, represented by two orbs, begin to Venn-diagram only to slip into total eclipse. Their longing for an end like the sun behind him lighting the sponge and plate in his hands. When he puts them together, he sees in his reflection what he has never seen but knows is his face. Ivory plumage. A thick, pointed bill. *I'm going to need a long neck*, he thinks, *to elongate the moment when I pick out my death from the weeds.*

Definite Article

The back is the definite article of the body.
There is no back in nature, no hindquarters. Everything faces you,
but you do not have the combination. The face is a vault
that is rumored to hide shelter, a warm compress.
Or there is only a solitary fly that startles when the face is opened.
The face of your beloved is a vault that you have opened.
There are monsoons that close the world off to anything
that isn't rain. Here, on the ground is the secret door
I have demarcated with the personal pronoun. I was entrusted with
the front of my body, which keeps having flashbacks
to when it was a part of experience.

Bellfounding

Before the world, nothing
was side-by-side,
so no two things could be
compared or wished for
or become. Stars
had yet to function
in myth: there doesn't
have to be truth,
just what we want
to glean from the whole
place lowered
over the mold
and clamped together,
bronze pouring
between us
and what we know,
pouring mouthward
into a cave
that can be rung against
the walls of a mountain,
itself a mold
the sky falls upon
as the present falls
upon the past, the samurai
falls upon his sword.
You hold out for me,
you wait by the ocean's
obfuscating grave
whose roiling echo
recalls the cargo of Zong, whose
voice are we to follow
or did we follow

and when did you start
speaking in sun
through the fingers the trees
lace in front of my eyes.
Your voice was once dark—
I know this
because I can see
with just what I remember
of you
when you were my parents
and when you were Agamben
you told me, *the only evil*
consists instead in the decision
to remain in a deficit of existence,
so you lifted the bell
and the soil stayed there,
though nothing now
is where you left it.

Caedmon

I sit with my head in my hands, turned
against everything. I'm facing what I think

is the wind. It has the eyes I've sought,
the skin I've felt under stone. It has

the sound of only and a wrist of land.
I can smell it calling through swirling

birch. And when I reply, my voice
estranges me, praises this blindfold

of world across my eyes. Dark felt
making my eyelashes bow. What I find

here will be represented, broken
and exposed. What I say will have

ruin value contained in the breath
of a body that is maddeningly whole.

Degree of Nothing

Let one not fool you, we're subject to worlds
and they pull on the eye with their gravities.

I sway past persons calling me home.
There is no one home. I am walking to another,

I am walking down the corridor
like water fills whatever this is. Burning me

when I touch it, its slender face carved by wind
is addressed by a face it cannot see.

Mountains are made so that things fall off.
When I fell at your feet you weren't there.

I wasn't going to listen to my voice,
but then I thought maybe it was yours.

Maybe the front of this building is the side
I'm on. The hull of a body can be a shore

or a zero, every zero wraps around
like an echo, a prodigal son. As I walk inside

the zero, there is a concentration of everything
I end up calling leaves.

Previously Forgotten

Notes toward a pre-forgotten literature should include
a consideration of the conditions under which forgottenness
occurs—who performs the forgetting in favor of what is
remembered in its place, if there was a game or festivity
that pulled on the mind, which parent, deceased, the literature
belonged to and, if the title page is inscribed, if it can be erased
in favor of a light pencil jotting of the reduced price, also
if such an inscription is kept, could it be smiled *down upon*
by a stranger who doesn't know its pre-forgotten provenance
with both the inscription and lightly jotted price already
yellowed by the sun—the pages will have to be pre-aged—
since this yellowing would indicate either use,
if, say, the literature was left on a windowsill, brushed
aside by a particularly injurious thought or telephone ring,
or non-use if it had been placed on a bookshelf negligently
positioned in the sun's daily path. A pre-forgotten literature
should also include a mustiness of smell—it is, after all,
a tangible embodiment of time's passing, pre-passed—
and privilege, since "previously forgotten" implies an earlier state
of attention (toward an author and content of probable
maleness), though author and content are variables
of lesser consequence, since attention is to be fleeting,
just so long as to have checked the box in either
the public or personal realm—the pencil can only hold
one body at a time, the tail has only one dog, etc.
Emphasis should be placed on forgottenness, which doesn't care
how long one's attention is held, how long the underline
props its *fill-in-the-blank*; meanwhile a trace of it should be
pre-left, just enough as to imply *no trace*—an abstract, say,
written in academic obliqueness, its link dead or behind
a subscription wall, the password for which has been extinguished
or requires an obsolete special character, some combination
of symbol and movement—and evidence of the author's forthright

belief in the content at hand tamped into language,
into the golem of language called tone, which should ring
in the ear as if an ear had briefly caught it, or as if
such a tone were like the phallus of a waterfowl
attempting to curl into the vaginal space of zeitgeist
continuously in the process of evolving new swerves
of musculature so as to stay ahead of tone, ahead of the author's
falling behind lurking in the background of the background
in perpetuity, self-solidifying, trapping itself there
under language without a shiv to sever its limb,
making the *failure to do so* physical, giving it ligaments
still banding locations of the body together, insufferably
described as "between-the-lines" as if a magnifying glass
were the lone item that could reveal hidden barnacles
of intention just below the surface of language
if only the reader were cunning and perceptive, the kind
of reader the author wishes could be a quick machete
through foliage away, but such foliage reveals itself
to be plastic, the machete, also plastic, the writing day's density
closing the avenues and shopwindows of projects
never started or completed, unveiling the only option
as found in the recesses of *same-old*, whatever that had been
festooned stuck shriveled like PLU stickers once removed
from the skin of produce, the literature also shriveled,
piled with its brethren under the intermittent spritzing
of chilled water or, rather, over a piece of masking tape
noting the genre, its edges using years to push off from the slab
of shelving, its dust jacket pre-dated, boxy in design
and with an image unambiguously representative of its title.
If a literature can skip right to this spot before it is written,
before trouble is spent on the part of publicists (who are
themselves like salmon attempting to jump a little waterfall
only to flop into the open mouth of a bear), before

traffic is braved by family members and friends on the way
to a reading, sparsely attended, before the author reads
what has trundled onto the screen and sits back,
before all this, when the desire to be remembered is spied
from afar, its shape and form fuzzy, and is misidentified as
anything but—then, perhaps, a literature wouldn't need to be
authored insofar as authorship constitutes *labor* or *birth*,
it wouldn't be an infant—at any moment—about to be smothered
amidst the resounding sound of crickets of no or bad press.
It would be pre-smothered, already unable to hold itself up,
but *on purpose* and with the conviction of *not* having to entail
the problems of others like an overturned hermit crab,
its flesh fodder for literature trying to capitalize its "L"
in order to be *looked back on* or anthologized, such failed
attempts embroidered into the marrow of the idea
that inspires the idea, which isn't to say pre-forgottenness
would reflect insularity, not entirely, or promote it
like the metal-grated windows of garden-level apartments
behind which authors scribble freely in the margins,
a literature, pre-forgotten, would contain only margins
so that they wouldn't be margins anymore, the whole page
would be marginalia of lesser or afterthought, or who knows
what secrets, notes toward this literature would have to inquire
into the potential for immortality in the margins
via the fingers of famed authors, long deceased or living
as if he or she is long deceased, and leaving examples
of penmanship behind to be discovered by an executor
or scholar combing the stacks for some forgotten literature
a famed author admired or pilfered, which is to say
as the repository for others is the only kind of afterlife.

Multiverse

Somewhere you are a hydria being pulled across the water.
Villagers are thirsty and waiting for you
to return in whose hands those are, her image
obscured by the sun. You assume it is a woman,
which is why you are a hydria, but not one
featuring red- or black-figure technique
adumbrating a scene of encounter, a white flower
of cotton either given or received.
You are the color and texture of material
the woman—now I am assuming—shaped
with a combination of hands and fire and clay,
then left out in exposure to dry. Samaras of maple,
which had previously whirled, are now krill
to the baleen at the mouth of you, tipped
until you are full or maybe the woman
notices and skims the samaras aside.

Ruin Value

There is the history of night in each night
I spend here allowing
lowercase sand to spill from me.
My fingers open despite my mind.
To spite my mind, my voice
does not remember
crossing the river to your ear
where the other side keeps whatever it finds
in the black water.
Do not worry. The other side
will lift you and change you
if how you were standing
doesn't make it across.

Passaic, Speaking

Looking elsewhere
        as I have,

                I look now
at a brown mallard

        drooping down
                its gray tendons

into me,
        drinking from my waist

                and pelvis,
the slope and scoop

        of where I was
                under cover

of stars and moon,
        vessels

                wearing away
what they carry

        each time they are
seen.

                As echo of origin,
held breath,

        you lean over me
                consisting,

peering between
        muscle and form.

                You find I
peer back.

        I have a need
            to lie here

as though on a surgical table,
        flowing

              as I present
my undulating body

        for you
            to find your

falsehoods
       in my eyes.

Their Papers

The day is a day now that I've sat on the branches
above the aging crocodiles, taunted them
with my libidinous song. The secret is in marking time,

marking the many snaps of the crocodiles' jaws,
and how far the sounds travel in this watery muck.
Across the street are lawyers and law clerks,

doctors and assistants to the world's gray empire
docking overnight. They watch me folding
my wrinkled clothes, their brows furrowing

past skin and bone and mind. What does it say
on their papers? Am I meeting or exceeding expectations,
or has some variant appeared like a Christ?

I remember this morning like it was yesterday,
when the mares were just foals and the foals
had just passed between rails of a fence

their uninhabited dreams. I remember sleeping
with you, blue night, in your redundancy,
letting my lids droop their delirious thoughts

like what a plane I've been, pulling an interminable sun.
I remember the locust as the locust would, awakened
and restrained by the pestilence and judgment

vibrating its translucent wings. And I remember
picking up a locust shell to try to find the wings.
We force men into circles, make them slaves.

Peace Epic

I had to pick up arms in order to put them down. Had to know

their weight, their cold or heat or mixture. Left by other hands,

which held them last, which were mine. Had I made these arms.

Divined them out of metal. From the fire, which is accomplice

to the vulnerable part of space. Even sheathed it comes in contact.

The inner circle has to touch the outer to widen stone.

To form the edges of the lake. Where it begins and dirt begins,

crossing border with every lap. There has to be in the air a path

an arm has made. And a wake in preparation. Waiting to show

the past. A point we can depart from, sharpens. Its roundness

falls away. And what we grasp is later come before. To guide

our arms into the furnace. To stay there long enough to count.

How many of us are or will become objects. That speak

in an object's voice. Coming not from the mouth. There is no

from an object. Nor to. There is no *to* another. But how

we become objects we do not understand. Understands us.

And follows us. Has its hand on the direction of our back.

We go to where no longer is. Not wreckage, which signals

still present in the mind. Nor the figments of wreckage called

trace. We can trace our arms back to intention. To being. Arms

make our hands legible. Read them. Tell me what they have

done. To make us hold them. First, material. History woven

from the plural. Then the strands that cross over, cross over.

Into another category. Into an object. The part in the city's hair.

Is parted by a body left to move. To be parted with.

Degree of Nothing

I know all too well the things
things have done. In the past,
the calendars were new. The lake
kept going against itself.

A sailor stood up in his boat.
I wanted to be the wind.
And the others that stood
were oblivious. They held

onto the idea of oblivion.
They were minds in that way.

Black Paintings

Fight with Cudgels (Francisco Goya, 1819–1823)

To collapse means to crumble but also to compress
remnants into the remembrance of a whole
body, this person was. Now it is broken
into its swinging and what it swings. A cudgel
that continues its arc to strike another
face turning it to the other side of the coin.
Can it be this gets him closer to the assemblage of his legs
that began pieced together to prop him up?
Even living with a right arm he has a feeling of the left
that was severed by the assemblage of a dam
at his elbow that portions out the flow
of the forearm and the upper arm. The cudgel. And the hand
is swinging severed because it is loosed by what it does.
The sentence describing violence has no words.

Saturn Devouring His Son (Francisco Goya, 1819–1823)

The corroded old doorknob comes off in my hand
like the sentence comes off in my eyes. As I read,
I am removing the head from the page,
my sight trailing off in dull sudden.
The dark has a tendency to do what light does,
to offset its subject, give it a voice
to emerge from as if that voice were landscape.
We live in this landscape because we live out
our days as the body that Saturn lifts up
to his mouth not moving, but moving unmoved
by our plea to remit, repay what we lost
of our limbs that were loaned to us at birth.
We determine the value of a thing
by how much we owe to those who remove it.

A Pilgrimage to San Isidro (Francisco Goya, 1819–1823)

Order is to progression as order is to rest
in our reliance on things as they are, as you arrange us
and so we must act out our placement accordingly,
we breathe what we are—this pilgrimage curling like a wisp
of pipe smoke creating demand
for a nose to inhale it, a crowd to inhabit the individual
person, what are you but your ration for today
of things happening without your knowledge, in your name?
You lead me not out of myself, but further in
to where I brought myself with these arms
if you would return them. This mouth could yawn
open, could be a cave for the song that travels
by wind to hollow out the face. But let it, Chris.
You have to let it.

Rejoinder

There have been physical impediments to forsaking my name.
I look in the mirror and the mirror lies.
I lie every time I put on my eyes.
The wind whirls down its color into clothes,
resembling the way it whips through the legs
that grieve giving birth to us,
pushing inscrutability into leaves
that are tossing somewhere, somewhere on the line.
It is always the line that hangs me.
Wrings my head into a bucket of loam.
My head is still here and I'm faithful to it.
Faithful to a fault. And the mirror when it turns
disappears into no more answers.

Schedule for Burning

The sea consumed by anxious gulls
is the sound I hear on the dark surface of things.
I follow what I call my soul
to the shore where a bonfire rages,

fronds and scraps of weed
cast off as if they were a burden.
One of us comes back from gathering, arms
full of the arms of trees,

which we sling through sleeves
to scare off what we imagine hunts us.
We know others are here
because we hear, because we haven't had a meal

and hear with our stomachs.
I can just reach over and grasp the dark air
and the dark air obliges. I can lie down
if I want to and the sand will adjust

its tongue. It isn't so bad,
this night among many,
this break in the reign of the sun.
We get to lean into the fire

to find the fire on our faces. We get to grasp
a part of an indefinite figure
and picture the whole it's a part of,
ribbons of the night's black hair.

We get to stay up past burning, linger
in the breath of the fire, which we inhale
and love, having wayward love
and so much of it that it turns inward

and is lost. Friend, if you are there,
come to meet me. I am drifting devoured.
I am ready to say goodnight.
Come meet me so I can release it.

Beach Scene

I wake up here.
Like I'm inside a shell
boiled open
to other people.
Laughing. Angling
themselves against
the waves. Some have
the look of people
I'd see on the street.
Others are here
because there's room.
When I turn to you,
I am as much myself
as where I'll go.
So far I've gone
nowhere. I've woken
up. I've fed on the air
rising out of this oven.
I walk to the others.
Still laughing. Still angling
against the faded water.
Faded by the choices
of the artist. Faded as if
the artist were squinting
for us. Pawned for
something only needed
in the moment. They
have green faces
that curl like aging leaves.
They jump like green spiders.

Lean beneath their skins.
Lean like the air is lean
and hollow. They have
corymbs of Spanish lime
in their hair, luring me
further and further in.
I don't know what I'm doing.
The water finds its way
above my eyes.

Layer of Ash

Even the air is freestanding, not sitting

on any one fixture, but all of them

and none of them, simultaneously,

one at a time.

Look skyward:

the algae that floats on the surface

of the ocean is sky to fish and mollusk,

to divers who wrap their hose into a loop

and unspool it as they descend

between ideograms depicting darkness

(the grace
of the water
is the wind)

and darker still, tiny eyes aglow

in their context. When ambient

pressure collapses the diver's suit,

when the windshield seems to wrinkle

with ash, when it coats the landscape

with leaving

the house nearby, full of looseness,

you wave your hand and the small piles

itself into the breeze, handfuls of dirt cast

into where the coffin will be.

This room is an H.

I walk one side I know

not which, profane space

all the way up to the perpendicular corridor,

sacred in its purpose as the path to concurrency,

this hollow letter short of where light can be

thrown or not at all.

(This room is an H inside of a bird.
Inside of the bird are the changing leaves.
Inside of this minute, winter.)

I take it personally:

the squirrels loping half-moons,

the half-moons referencing in the night,

which is a day I remember.

I was hoping the leaves would brush the top of me

as I passed.

What does the bird say?

What *does* the bird say?

[I Speak into the Color Blue Cut]

I speak into the color blue cut

from the sepia cloth

speak into the night

dangling from the trees

each word cut from your words

yours truly on a horse

rearing up to say something

like glass I followed here

through spangled birch bark

though headless and footless

all the way down

I have to grow a blue world

I have to surrender soluble

to the parallel strokes

I have to make damned sure

I get it right this time

ruins in reverse

putting themselves together

then falling from my arms

held over the fire

and melting into this line

and this

is how I treat you, rare bird

I have a problem with all of this suddenly

stopped, all of this quiet

I should speak you into being

I should speak myself across

separate leaves

into *bough* that comes out *now*

from my mouth

[Your Words Trail Off above Me into Radial Space]

Your words trail off above me into radial space

the same on the left as it is

in your hair

my head held out before me

a lantern

my hands also lanterns

carried by reflection into trees

I sit beneath

shoving food into the hole in my neck

shoving my neck into the hole in the sky

the same on the left as it is

upright

I must live upright

I must not be a screen

but the screen's sudden crows

enough sense to follow

not behind but alongside

what they know

Valuing

This hole in the ground
is where I've stepped, not knowing
the ground would save it—
shallower or deeper depending
on the weight: a value of impression.
There are tiny pocks where sand stuck
and lifted with my foot. And then
there are other people making other
holes in the ground. They trail after me
in shallows like a snake. Moving
like an arm moves to pull me out of sleep.
I dreamt that I was only, one
of one. I dreamt that I could tell you
and you would know.

Pastorale

The sky tries to lure me underground,
but the ground needs to open
for me to fall for it. A precedent, maybe,
but there isn't precedent.
Or maybe an apple needs to fall
now that fall is a word I've used.
Time needs to pass, that's for sure.
And I need to age. I need to love
and fall in love like an apple
shot out of a seed. Just in case,
I have a convenient packet
and a can held up to my ear.
Words whisper themselves
without the string. And when I whisper back,
it's a lie pulling breath behind it.
But there aren't enough lies to go around,
enough wind to whip them back
to my eyes, which do not believe
even when I see, which isn't often.

Degree of Nothing

The face beyond the eyes is the book beyond the hands.
I cannot open what I perceive to be a limit.
When you are before me, I am last, lasting.
I live as long as you are singing.

The end is a passage through another's face.
Your eyes are two paths I could take.
Mouth is a river pushing out. And upstream,
the bed where I was spawned.

You live in the other like a snail in a shell.
I lost my ears trying to hear you.
Worn to smooth skipping rocks,
shores recede to the sound of the waves.

I discern what you can from fallible clouds
and affix it to both of our bodies.
I am going to brush the hair of this valley.
When I close my eyes, everything gets louder.

Trust

Sleeping is the only way to demonstrate trust. You must find a formation and rest the mind against it. While sleeping, you are vulnerable. Small excuses could crawl on you. Reasons, with their rapaciousness, could flit away with your change. Though the world appears to retain its shape, it doesn't have the constitution not to. The sleeping you did as a child doesn't count. Your parents unfolded trust from its cloth napkin. Your sister would wake you by asking if you were awake. Neither can you, by pretending to sleep, pretend to demonstrate trust. The eyes can be *too* closed. In the humid season, doors make an unpleasant, unsticking sound by swelling at the hinges. You cannot sneak through your life.

Porousness

It is good to make the most of being money. A coin in the palm never leaves the hand. It takes us into the pockets and purses of others. We see into so few windows. Even with the drapes open and the scene we're peering at leaning on the sill. We can't see the action people make. We can't taste their meal. We can't find the spoon they seem to be serving with. It isn't in the air we are privy to. You try to flip yourself over to the side with the face. You try to spin without the hand to spin you. Sun behind the buildings—you don't glint anymore. *Why don't we glint in the moonlight?* you ask, but the meal is over and the plates have paintings on them.

Devouring Each Other

When I was a child, I lived your childhood.
I swept the rooms you swept in and out
the grooves in the boards. I held the paintbrush

and kissed your sweetheart at eleven, at fifteen,
metal-scent ringing in my ears all true, all true.
At eighteen, I attended your institution and

learned from your mistakes, which were old to me,
worn by having been made. Your infant peered
into my eyes, absent for recognizing little

yet percolating with continuous instance.
At eighty, I was eighty. At ninety, I was ninety.
When you died, we died and I kept on living.

Object Permanence

The idea of god displaces the current
life in favor of the next. This isn't the real
shore or the real water leaning
against it like the book between them has been removed.
The real is the angle of absence, or so you
say. I am on the sand. I am with my wife,
daughter and dog. It is some version of dwindling
light. We are wearing heavier clothes,
and the object the dog has been retrieving
is thrown onto a patch of water
water collapses around as if it were the hinge
of some carnivorous plant. Into which
the point of retrieval spills until it has passed
without the *she* of the dog noticing,
but my wife notices and tries to pull the point
closer by swimming farther out
after the dog, she comes after, becomes the second
side of some constellation I'll someday ascribe them to,
infrequent in sky from the privilege
of sand, which is where our daughter keeps
the blanket from catching in the wind. There, now, is
my wife in the process of out and my daughter
in the process of on *this* shore that solidifies
as the *t* falls away so that I feel *his*
wife drowning and *his* daughter unable to
survive if I swim out, if I risk saving and fail
to retain my adherence to this world—
the same world that sends feedlot into the car when we drive
to your previous midwestern body, the same
that gives me the ability to recoil
when I get too close to what would turn out
the fabric of my hippocampus like a pocket,

and the same that accretes in inverse proportion
to my experience of it that's left
a part of the water encroaching is what your body displaces
closer to my feet as if spread by the broad edge
of a butter knife—the lone stoplight asking us to pause
before proceeding, the dilapidated street
at the end of which, your parents—spreading toward me
in the water a color I could never describe,
not for lack of shedding the words from my mind
now impinged upon by the cry of my daughter
being pecked at by the cry of gulls
until I can't hear her any more
than the sound of my body dislodging into ocean.

Remonstrance

I survive myself on the street under the dome of echo hung there.
I survive myself skinny, that I had strayed and felt torn.
I survive myself in the morning, morning says.
Survive each evening as the evening comes on.
I survive the loosely knitted only to stop at tightly wound,
beyond which I survive myself solid again.
I watch myself survive at the end of a letter.
I watch through the portal by surviving my sight.
I am seized by survival. I sting with it.
I feel a constant emerging-from-the-abyss.
I feel a stone still stone in still smaller form.
I am desperate to die. I start by surviving.

Placeholder

I've placed this
inside the envelope
I slipped beneath
the door to many
years from now
when I no longer
coincide with myself,
when I've forgotten
what I've chosen
not to remember
and I may or may
not have witnessed
what I've seen,
when what I had
been doing without
realizing it was aging
the world, using a trowel
to apply aging, its
thick putty filling
chinks in the surface,
smearing them with
beams of light (*see also:*
time) that chinks
can also refer to,
so that no room
could pass through
the lack of room left
for me to age
meant ensuring
that I not be present
even in presence,
that my constant evaluating
be a twine strung

from being to being
here (I would pull on
the *e* and feel *val*
at my palm before
the twine would
fray and burst),
I'll open to where
this has been holding
the page beneath it,
the real page
with the real poem
I was never able
to write because
I thought it could
be written, I'll recall
how I had to allow
things to happen
before they could,
how my need to control
diminished my capacity
to withstand even
the frailest iteration
of change, how I
often reached into
the myriad of π
expecting to pull
the same number,
the same lock of
the door I'll find
this under
keyed to waxing
or waning crescent.

Passaic, Again

Also, I must capture you in song. I must find music to set to this
aging and follow the river to my death. But it isn't at the end,
the Passaic says, now speaking, it is at the disappearance

of words, which have guided you here. Sometimes when I quote
from what is etched into walls, I permit myself liberties, in the first
place, happiness, which means failing, invoking the terrible cloak.

Wear it in good conscience (Passaic, again). Wear it around me
completely on the banks and shoals and muddy spots of steppes.
We zoomed in, Passaic and I, under the rocks and hidden machinery,

and the English language balled up in our hands like hair.
I didn't know what to say. I didn't say it true or false, breath
or wind. I trimmed a piece from you and kept it boxed.

Years later and with a kind of unraveling motion, I hold you
and am holding you now—a dark is grounding birds,
deterring snakes that I remember vividly for how they tasted

of mirrors. On the other side was written a jot, tossed off
to convince discoverers of its little care that wind would wind
its toy heart set beating. It read, "Soon after my tutor died,

I numbed, then felt a kind of leaving so strong I knew not
that I would soon have fewer possessions than I do now."
No possessions, I thought, what a solitary nun.

They (sentences) have architecture for conversion.
If I wanted to believe in burning beacons, I would say so.
I would wait for those who know what beacons signify:

alone. Let me eat no more, nor find you as beautiful
as the day we were married. You make it more difficult,
more like staying when I know I have to fade.

Acknowledgments

Grateful acknowledgment is made to the editors of the following publications where versions of these poems (some with different titles) first appeared: *32 Poems*, "Remonstrance"; *American Letters & Commentary*, "Layer of Ash"; *Boston Review*, "Devouring Each Other"; *California Journal of Poetics*, "Passaic, Again," *Cimarron Review*, "Passaic, Speaking," "Valuing"; *Colorado Review*, "Rejoinder"; *Conjunctions*, "Black Paintings," "Peace Epic"; *Crazyhorse*, "Degree of Nothing" (1); *Cream City Review*, "Caedmon"; *Green Mountains Review*, "Bellfounding," "Dwelling"; *Gulf Coast*, "Asylum," "Clearing"; *Handsome*, "Degree of Nothing" (3), "Orientation"; *Harvard Review*, "Definite Article"; *Iowa Review*, "Division of Labor," "Multiverse," "Placeholder," "Ruin Value"; *Kenyon Review*, "Geometry of Echo"; *Paris-American*, "Pastorale," "Schedule for Burning," "Their Papers"; *Poetry Northwest*, "Trust"; *Sixth Finch*, "Beach Scene," "Degree of Nothing" (2); *Third Coast*, "Map of Belonging"; *TYPO*, "Object Permanence"; *Vinyl*, "Porousness"; *Word For/Word*, "[I Speak into the Color Blue Cut]," "[Your Words Trail Off above Me Into Radial Space]."

"Division of Labor," "Multiverse," "Placeholder," and "Ruin Value" received the Iowa Review Award for Poetry, selected by Srikanth Reddy. "Pastorale," "Schedule for Burning" and "Their Papers" received the Paris-American Reading Series Prize. Thank you to Srikanth Reddy and to the editors of these publications.

My thanks as well to Moonassi for permitting me to use his incredible artwork, and to Susan Howe for allowing me to borrow the following language from *Spontaneous Particulars: The Telepathy of Archives* (New Directions, 2014): "you permit yourself liberties—in the first place—happiness."

I would like to thank my teachers and friends for their counsel, keen attention, and support, especially Kanika Agrawal, Alexis Almeida, Dan Beachy-Quick, Julie Carr, George David Clark, Lindsey Drager, Graham Foust, Yanara Friedland, Elisa Gabbert, Eryn Green, Samuel Clare Knights, David Kutz-Marks, Joe Lennon, Poupeh Missaghi, TaraShea Nesbit, Susannah Nevison, Bin Ramke, Broc Rossell, Siobhán Scarry, Eleni Sikelianos, and Robert Yerachmiel Sniderman.

My eternal gratitude to Jericho Brown for believing in this collection. Thank you to Beth Dial and the National Poetry Series, and to Bethany Snead and everyone at the University of Georgia Press for helping to make all this possible.

Finally, this book would not have happened without the boundless support of my family. Michelle and Thalia: every one of these poems is dedicated to you.